Steve Parish

DISCOVERING AUSTRALIAN

BIRDS

A LITTLE AUSTRALIAN GIFT BOOK

www.steveparish.com.au

DISCOVERING AUSTRALIAN BIRDS

At dawn, the vast continent of Australia resounds to bird calls. The "bushman's alarm clock", the Laughing Kookaburra, chuckles and whoops, butcherbirds warble, magpies carol and from the treetops come the sweet, high-pitched songs of smaller birds. As the sun rises, its rays shine brightly upon some of the world's most remarkable feathered creatures, from tiny jewelled cameos of fairy-wrens and rainbow-coloured parrots to stately waterbirds, regal eagles and the magnificent flightless Emu.

Some bird lovers travel the length and breadth of Australia adding to an ever-growing list of new species seen. However, most people just enjoy looking at birds, enjoying their beauty and being amazed by their behaviour. It is not necessary to endure hardships or spend a fortune to see Australia's birds, for they are all around, in bushland, wetland or forest, on the seashore, in heathlands, on plains and even in cities and towns.

The main requirements for enjoying birds are open eyes and open ears. Sit quietly in the open air wherever you may be, and sooner or later birds will come to you.

Title page:
Eclectus Parrot

Opposite:
Crimson Rosella

A GRACEFUL SYMBOL

The Black Swan was one of the first Australian birds to be discovered by Europeans, and today is one of the world's best-known waterfowl.

Black Swans are splendid parents to their downy cygnets, escorting them as they feed on water plants and defending them vigorously against predators.

Opposite:

Black Swan and cygnet

Left:

Black Swan

GALAHS

The Galah is a medium-sized cockatoo, whose numbers have increased since graziers and farmers provided supplies of water and grain for its use. After the nesting season, flocks of Galahs fill the skies with rose and silver feathers as they circle and swoop before descending on a trough or waterhole. Once perched, they interact playfully, raising their crests, preening their mates and even hanging upside down while screeching loudly.

Opposite
and right:
Galahs

AERIAL PREDATORS

The hooked bills and large, keen eyes of the two birds shown here identify them as predators. The Wedge-tailed Eagle can take prey as large as small kangaroos, but is most often seen dining on a rabbit or a roadkill. The Brown Falcon is a long-legged opportunist, as happy catching tiny grasshoppers as picking up a small snake or lizard. When summer brings bushfires, Brown Falcons may be seen on the ground, patrolling the edges of a burning area, snatching up prey as it flees the flames.

Opposite:

Wedge-tailed Eagle

Left:

Brown Falcon

TWO SPECTACULAR COCKATOOS

Australia is the land of parrots and cockatoos. Many are brightly coloured, but the Yellow-tailed Black-Cockatoo and Sulphur-crested Cockatoo are sombre black and dazzling white respectively. While the Sulphur-crested Cockatoo is comparatively common, many black-cockatoos are becoming increasingly rare.

Opposite:

Sulphur-crested Cockatoo

Left:

Yellow-tailed Black-Cockatoo

REEF STALKERS

Egrets are long-legged, long-necked waterbirds that stalk the shallows stabbing or snapping up fish and other water creatures. In the breeding season, they grow beautiful plumes on their heads and backs.

The Eastern Reef Egret is unusual because it frequents salt water, feeding on small fish living around coral or rocky reefs. Its chicks are reared in a nest built on a coral cay or island.

Opposite:
**Eastern
Reef Egret**

Right:
**Eastern Reef
Egret in flight**

AUSTRALIAN PELICANS

The Australian Pelican is a superb flier that may travel tremendous distances at high altitudes. It becomes tame at seaside resorts, but prefers to nest far inland on the shores of isolated salt lakes. Here chicks fledge in a race against time, for all too soon the shallow waters will dry up and the fish on which the pelicans feed will disappear. Then the flocks must fly to new wetland homes.

Opposite:

Australian Pelicans

Left:

Australian Pelican in flight

AUSTRALIA'S ROBINS

Early British visitors to Australia nostalgically named small scarlet-breasted birds "robins", although they were not related to the Old World robins. Other birds were given names that relate to their appearance or habits.

Opposite:
Jacky Winter

Right:
Male Scarlet Robin

LORIKEETS

High-pitched calls overhead call attention to fast-flying lorikeets travelling on whirring wings from one blossom-laden tree to another. These brilliantly coloured small parrots lick up nectar with brush-tipped tongues. While doing so, they become dusted with pollen, which they transfer to the next bouquet of flowers they visit.

Opposite:
Rainbow Lorikeet

Left:
Scaly-breasted Lorikeet

GROWING UP ON A CORAL CAY

Birds that depend on the sea for a living, such as tropicbirds, terns, boobies and noddies, find coral cays convenient places to rear their chicks. While the chick is small, one parent may remain to shield it from the heat of the sun while the other parent is off fishing at sea.

Opposite:

Red-tailed Tropicbird and chick

Left:

Black Noddy and chick

MAGPIES AND BUTCHERBIRDS

Australia is the home of a black and white brigade of birds with outstanding choral talents. Magpies gather in family parties and carol to greet the dawn. Butcherbirds have clear, ringing songs, which often incorporate mimicry of other birds' calls.

Opposite:

Australian

Magpie

Right:

Pied

Butcherbird

SPOONBILLS

Spoonbills wade through shallow water, snapping up small creatures with their remarkable bills. These long-legged birds are devoted mates and dedicated parents who share nesting duties. They affectionately preen their mates and chicks with delicate nibbling motions of their huge beaks.

Opposite:
**A pair of
nesting
Yellow-billed
Spoonbills**

Right:
**Spoonbills on
the mudflats**

LAUGHING KOOKABURRA

Kookaburras are giant members of the kingfisher family. However, while they will splash into ponds and pools to seize fish, kookaburras usually live in open bushland, where they dive on reptiles and other small creatures. The kookaburra carries its prey back to its perch and bashes it against a branch before gulping it down. The Laughing Kookaburra's call resembles human mirth, and is often produced by a family group shrieking in chorus.

Right:

**Laughing
Kookaburra**

BLUE-WINGED KOOKABURRA

The call of this northern kookaburra is raucous and maniacal. The best time to hear the call is at dawn, when it resounds along riverbanks and billabongs. Like its southern relative, the Blue-winged Kookaburra lives in family groups. A mated pair nests in a hollow branch or hole in a river bank, then their offspring from previous nestings assist in feeding the chicks.

Left:

Blue-winged Kookaburra

KINGFISHERS

Kingfishers are big-headed, long-billed, short-tailed birds. Their plumage is often vividly hued in reds, blues or greens. Australia's kingfishers include bushland dwellers, such as the Forest Kingfisher, that catch insects and small reptiles for food. They often nest in holes in termite nests in trees.

Other kingfishers, including the Azure Kingfisher, are more conventional feeders, darting into water to take small fish, tadpoles or crustaceans. Their chicks are usually raised in holes in river banks.

Opposite:
Forest Kingfisher

Left:
Azure Kingfisher

KINGS OF THE BUSHLAND

Australian King-Parrots are often seen in family parties. A brilliant male with a glorious scarlet head and breast will escort a mainly green female and several youngsters.

These gorgeous parrots nest in hollows in trees. They eat seeds and fruits, and readily come to garden feeders.

Opposite:
Male
Australian
King-Parrot

Right:
Female
Australian
King-Parrot

INDEX

Right:

Malleefowl